@ WHAT COST?

A GRIPPING

EXAMINATION

OF THE PRICE

FOR REDEMPTION

BISHOP
ERIC A. LAMBERT, JR.

outskirts
press

Outskirts Press, Inc.
http://www.outskirtspress.com

ISBN: 978-1-9772-3255-7

Library of Congress Control Number: 2020916567

PRINTED IN THE UNITED STATES OF AMERICA

INTRODUCTION

S alvation is free, and we should receive it with joy. I am sure many of you have heard this significant announcement. Yes, redemption, adoption, and all our Father offers is free to us. Have you ever thought about the price God paid to adopt us. What steps did He take to reveal His heart of love and provide salvation for all of us?

Like so many people, we enjoy the ride without thinking about the costs. Like the person who rides in the car, they do not know of the price of the gas, as they just enjoy the transportation. Now, I do not suggest the cost is complicated or burdensome to God. Every action, even a God action has a consequence, whether good or bad.

When I was working toward my master's degree in forensic psychology, I spent, many days and nights reading, writing, and studying. The cost of that degree was hard work while working as a full-time pastor. The number of papers written and the reading of various textbooks and journals was exhausting. Sometimes my eyes would not focus, and I just wanted to yell, "I quit!" With the help of the Holy Spirit, I completed my task with a GPA of 3.97, only three-tenths away from a perfect grade. When I look at my diploma and degree, I know what it cost!

Have you ever thought about the cost of all God has done for you? I hope you have and will continue to do so after reading this short book. I want you to think about the love of God, His desire to fellowship with His children, and the price He paid to bring you into His eternal Kingdom.

Jesus is the first person to introduce God as our Father. In the Old Testament, God was not viewed as a Father but a Holy God who punishes for sin and judges those who deserve it. This book examines God in the role of Father. I will focus on four distinct areas of this demonstration of Fatherhood by God. God desires a relationship with His children. He wants us to know what it means to have God as Father in our everyday life.

Enjoy the lessons ahead.

Grace and peace to all who read.

Bishop Eric A. Lambert, Jr.

> *"The LORD bless you and keep you; The LORD make His face shine upon you And be gracious to you; The LORD lift up His countenance upon you, And give you peace."*
> Numbers 6:24-26 (NKJV)

Dedicated to my Lord and Savior Jesus, the Christ of God. Without His help, nothing is possible.

TABLE OF CONTENTS

CHAPTER ONE

The Elder, To the elect lady and her children, whom I love in truth, and not only I, but also all those who have known the truth, because of the truth which abides in us and will be with us forever: Grace, mercy, and peace will be with you from God the Father and from the Lord Jesus Christ, the Son of the Father, in truth and love. I rejoiced greatly that I have found some of your children walking in truth, as we received commandment from the Father.

(2 John 1:1-4 NKJV)

GOD IS OUR FATHER

*Do not call anyone on earth your father; for
One is your Father, He who is in heaven.*
(Matthew 23:9 NKJV)

From the first verses in the Holy Bible, we are told how God created the heavens and the earth and everything in the world. "In the beginning, God created the heavens and the earth." (Genesis 1:1 NKJV) God is the creator of all things, including mankind. God is our creator. The beauty in the world, and the perfection of the union between the earth and the seas, reveals the mastery of the All-Mighty. As we see the balance between the sun, earth, moon, and stars, we know of His perfection. God is, by all understandings, the Master Creator. Yet, God is so much more than one who creates. To understand what it has cost God to be more than a creator, but also our Father, we must first consider the difference between the two.

Simply put, a creator creates. A creator begins with a thought or an idea and prepares a plan to bring this concept into reality. Gradually, the plan comes together, and the creation manifests as envisioned. In this, I am reminded of a sculpture. The creator looks at a mound of clay but does not merely see a pile of clay. They see beyond what it is and can envision what it will be. From this vision, they then create. With careful precision, every movement extends toward the ultimate creation. Adding and reducing where necessary, the creator is one with the process as they see their idea become a reality. They have created. They are creators! A child picks up a crayon and a piece of paper. What the child is envisioning is unknown to observers and, perhaps, to some extent, even to the child. Their concept of perfection differs from that of an adult, and yet they create. The colors magically transform the paper into some form of artwork that they continue to create until it looks exactly like what they have thought up. They have then created, and they are creators.

When we think of the term creation, it is easy to substitute the term, to make something. However, there is something more specific about creating than making something. Creating is more personal and individualized. Consider the difference between making a recipe and creating a dish. When we follow a recipe, we are making someone else's creation, or replicating what they have already created. However, when we add a dash of this or a teaspoon of that to achieve the exact taste that we have been imagining, then we create something new. While this difference may be subtle, it is important to understand that God did not simply make a world; He created it. He determined what would be, and out of nothing, He brought this concept into reality. He breathed life into the lungs of every living creature and provided a world that could sustain life for all those who would inhabit it. He did not replicate or follow a recipe. He did not seek examples, as there were none to be sought. He created, and He did so from the abyss of nothingness.

If a creator creates, then how is a father defined? A father creates life through conception, but he does not specifically mold the child to his own concept of what the child should be. A father may guide the child toward what he believes is in the child's best interest, but he does not eliminate all other options in such a way as to define the exact course for the child. I return to the example of the sculpture. Once the clay has been molded and dried, the creation does not change unless it becomes broken. Once the sculpture has been completed to the satisfaction of its creator, there is no need to make alterations or improvements. However, a father knows his child is continuously growing and changing. He knows the genetic structure of his child will inevitably mold the child into whatever they become. More importantly, even when the child's decisions are not the same as the father would have chosen for them, the father continues to love and nurture them. When the child falls, the father picks them up and wipes their tears, only to know that they will again fall in the future.

I fondly remember an instance when I was at a cricket match in the park. Cricket is a form of Jamaican baseball and the ball is made of solid wood. I was sitting next to my dad and the cricket ball was hit in my direction. The ball hit me on the ankle, and I tried to just take the pain. I heard my father say these words, "Rick, I know it hurts. You can cry if you want to cry." I laid my head on his shoulder and cried a bit. I think of God in this light. He invites us to come to Him as our Father and cry if we need to cry. The Apostle Peter teaches, "Casting all your care upon Him, for He cares for you." (1 Peter 5:7 NKJV) What a marvelous truth to hear. Our world causes pain and much suffering, and we Christians are not beyond the reach of pain. It is exciting to know we can bring all of our pain, anxiety, and sorrow to our Father, and He will help us.

A father takes the opportunities to guide the child and provide examples of how the child should avoid such injuries but remains aware that the child is learning and growing through these experiences. This means that the father does not remove all obstacles, but helps the child to learn how to overcome them. "Train up a child in the way he should go, and when he is old he will not depart from it." (Proverbs 22:6 NKJV) Training reaches the mind as well as the soul. Fathers are expected to train their children in the things of God so there will be a point of understanding when the great Father takes over the training. However, training is but one of the responsibilities of a father.

To define a father in the most simplistic terms is to state that a father is one who loves unconditionally and understands that all conditions will continuously change. Despite being in a position of control, a father does not control all conditions, but he hopes to prepare his family for the changes that may arise. Despite not being able to do everything for their family, a father provides the tools so they might do for themselves. I remember a childhood friend who wanted desperately to build a ramp for his bicycle just as he had seen on the television. His father had him to mow the lawn to earn the money for the lumber that he would need. My friend had this stack of two-by-fours and a sheet of plywood all ready to go. His father gave him a hammer, some nails, and a handsaw. He measured and drew out that ramp for about two weeks, looking at this stack of wood. His father asked him when he would build it, and he said that he was not sure if he could. I remember being over to visit when his father came out and told him he would never have a ramp built if he did not begin. He showed his father the completed drawing, and his father pointed out a few potential flaws. "How do I fix it?" my friend asked. His father walked away. Again and again he continued, until his father gave him a nod of approval. I remember this so vividly, as I wondered why his father had not told him how to fix his errors. Today, this friend is an engineer who can identify both flaws and ways to fix them because his father did not lead him, but he guided him.

A creator tells his creation what it will be, while a father provides the love and support to allow the child to become who they are. For the creator, the satisfaction comes in the creation's completion and the ability to bring their thoughts and ideas into reality. For the father, the satisfaction comes through watching the child change and develop. In both cases, the creation or the child is the primary source of joy and love. Yet, the love of a creator differs from that of a father. The creator loves the finished creation in its state of completion. Should the creation be broken or torn, then it is not repaired, but replaced with a new creation. The love is not unconditional. For a father, however, the expectation is knowing the child will have flaws. yet, the father knows the current state of the child is not the state of completion. There is no certainty in what the conditions will be in the future and yet, there is a love that can endure all changes. There is a reality that, without changes, the child is not growing and learning. For a father, there is a responsibility to ensure when changes occur, the child is able to move forward and grow. This leads to another significant difference. The creator determines the course of the creation and defines every detail. The father offers guidance but encourages the child to experience life and become the best version of themselves. In brief, the greatest difference between a creator and a father is that the former loves what they have done while the latter loves who their child becomes.

So, yes, God is our Creator as He created us and our world. He molded the universe with His own hands and defined the light and the darkness. With exact precision He considered what we would need to survive, and He ensured that all elements were in place for His creation. Yet, He became so much more than our Creator. He offered Himself as our Father. To understand what this cost Him, we must consider the consequences of being a father. If we were to ask many first-time fathers what it costs to be a father, we would get a lengthy list of items such as diapers, clothing, and food. We would hear about the lack of sleep and the toys scattered across the living room floor. They would probably add the loss of a social life and reduced free time to the list. Yes, fatherhood certainly forces changes upon those men. It would be difficult to argue with this line of thinking, as children are certainly expensive in today's society. However, what about the other costs? What are the consequences of being a father?

Being a father means knowing disappointments will come to the child and choosing to absorb the falls as much as possible. The realities of those disappointments are the consequences of opening one's heart up so much that you will experience the pain of loss and the fears of the unknown. Although a creator knows of the risk that their creation may become broken, they have the option to put it in a glass case and prevent any harms. A father, according to the father I spoke of, is that glass case. They try to protect and provide a resistance to the pain and suffering that life brings to their child. However, unlike a physical glass case, a father must be malleable, (pliable, bendable). They must be able to shift to meet the circumstances and adapt to the conditions. They must know when to change roles and when it is safe to break down. To look at a child and promise to love them unconditionally, accept their changes, and face their troubles with them and, in some instances, for them, is the essence of being a father. I find the consequences of this role in the moments when breaking down is not an option. Children need the love and support of their father. Our present society has done much to remove the sacredness of fathers. As we have become a matriarchal society, the position of father has become lost in the culture. I do not minimize the role of our gifted women, as their place is forever settled in Heaven. I do suggest that the role of the father has been watered down, and many of our children suffer because of it. Children need someone to cheer for them as well as provide the nurturing and guidance they will need as they grow in their present world. Children need protection, and it has always been the role of the father to provide protection.

When we read Psalm 91, it speaks of two interesting facts. One, the role of the father as a protector. The Psalmist declares: *"Surely he will save you from the fowler's snare and from the deadly pestilence. He will cover you with his feathers, and under his wings you will find refuge; his faithfulness will be your shield and rampart. You will not fear the terror of night, nor the arrow that flies by day, nor the pestilence that stalks in the darkness, nor the plague that destroys at midday. A thousand may fall at your side, ten thousand at your right hand, but it will not come near you." (Psalms 91:3-7 NIV)* The second fact is that this protection is relational. The protection is guaranteed to those who are connected to the father: "He who dwells in the shelter of the Most High will rest in the shadow of the Almighty. I will say of the LORD, "He is my refuge and my fortress, my God, in whom I trust." (Psalms 91:1-2 NIV). This protection is also given to those who love the Father. "Because he loves me," says the LORD, "I will rescue him; I will protect him, for he acknowledges my name. He will call upon me, and I will answer him; I will be with him in trouble, I will deliver him and honor him." (Psalm 91:14-15 NIV) So it is important to note that the passage does not simply address protection apart from relationship. This is what happens when we have full knowledge of the fatherhood of God. In fact, our children should feel the same protection from their fathers as they walk through life.

Although there are logical consequences of becoming

a father, there is also an abundance of joy. There are moments of video-game-playing and laughing through hard times. There are moments of pride and boundless love. Being the glass case for a creator means that you can ensure the creation's safety and be confident it will display the characteristics you intended. Being the same as a father means you absorb the pain, but you may choose to exercise limited control over your child's decisions. As God is the Creator, He could have easily placed the universe into a glass case and observed His creation exactly how He had envisioned. However, He did not. Instead, God offered Himself to us as our Father. He became more than our Creator, but He invites us to be called His children. He did not demand we remain precisely as He had intended but continues to keep His arms around us like a glass case and to embrace us with His love and guidance. He offered Himself as the one who would love us unconditionally and absorb the pain and suffering so we could grow and develop into who we are. He does not waver in His love for us when times are hard, and He does not turn away from us when we fall. Yet, why did God offer Himself to us as our Father?

Let us consider the frequency of the term "Father" throughout the teachings of Jesus. Jesus explained that He was the Son of God. "Then they all said, *are You then the Son of God? So He said to them, You rightly say that I am. (Luke 22:70 NKJV)* While one could stop there and state this meant God is Jesus's father, alone, especially as Jesus is the only Son of God. God is *the* Father, not *a* father. We do not refer him to as the creator of Jesus, but as the Father of Christ. This distinction shows that God did not want the relationship of a creator and a creation, but that of the Father and His children. Romans 8:14 teaches, *"for as many as are led by the Spirit of God, these are sons of God."* God had given mankind freedom of choice, so mankind could make choices and follow their own paths along the journey of life. This was part of the creation that God had envisioned. He did not create mankind as a static work of art, but as one able to change and experience the world created by the Father. Creation responds to the creator; however, using freedom of choice, humans sought to change creation and as a result we sometimes miss the original intent of the creator.

We can now understand why God offered Himself as our Father. With free will as part of our design, God knew we would need His guidance and patience and unconditional love. He knew we would face challenges which would require His help. He also knew there would be moments when we would not follow His directives and instructions. He knew we would fail at times, yet He provides the love of a father to nuture us and bring us to a place of victory. The Lord would use our defeated moments as the springboard to a better life with Him. He would have to move with us and expand as we did. His love would have to serve as the walls of our protection, and His presence would have to encompass our choices. In order for His creation to become what He had envisioned, He would have to be much more than a creator. He would have to be a father. Even more, He would have to be more than a father. He would have to be "THE" Father.

God chose to be our Father and to continue to love us even when we do not follow His guidance. He sees our drawings of ramps and He points out the flaws, just as my friend's father did. Yet, when we do not change our plans in response to His guidance, and we fall, He is still there to pick us up, wipe our tears, and encourage us to try again. He is the Father. I am sure we can all recall many times when we did not obey the voice of our Lord. Has He ever ridiculed you? Has He ever just cut you off or made you feel worthless? I am certain your answer will be a resounding no. Our Father never condemns His children. "Therefore, there is now no condemnation for those who are in Christ Jesus." (Romans 8:1 NIV)

As we have now come to understand that God offered Himself to us as our Father because that is the best way to protect His creation and to allow mankind to experience life through free will, the pressing question of what this choice has cost Him can now be considered. I heard of a story about a mother whose child asked why it was raining. The child asked if raindrops are tears from Heaven. The child asked why God was crying so much, and the mother said that God cries when people are mean to each other. While I understood that the mother was using this opportunity to teach her child about the importance of being kind to one another, I am certain she did not realize her lesson would benefit all who heard it. I had never considered the idea of God being saddened. I knew of God being angry and jealous, but the emotion of sadness had never really crossed my mind in this way. Does God cry when people are mean to one another? If that were true, then we would never see sunny days. The world can be very cruel, and people often forget the importance of being kind to one another. Disease, war, and natural disasters bring about pain and suffering. Children go without enough to eat and families are broken apart. There are many reasons for sadness on earth, but how are these experienced in Heaven? Does God experience the same consequences of fatherhood as mankind? I believe He feels what we feel. The Lord told Moses this when He called Moses to be the deliverer of the people of God: *And the LORD said: "I have surely seen the oppression of my people who are in Egypt, and have heard their cry because of their taskmasters, for I know their sorrows." (Exodus 3:7 NKJV)*

When considering these questions, I thought about the difference between being a father and being *the* Father. A father has one or more children, but typically a small number in modern society because of the financial costs of raising children. A father provides for the children for a period of approximately eighteen years, at which point the children are adults and financially responsible for themselves. A father continues to provide love and guidance until the time he (or the child) passes from this earth.

There are also those moments when our children decide it is time to leave home. This is a normal evolution in the life of the child. For the parents, however, I am sure this is a moment of pain and possibly excitement. In many instances, that pain may become unbearable for the parents. The parents may feel sadness. In that way, I believe God feels sad when His children leave the fellowship with Him. A father feels the pain that his child feels and is saddened when his child falls. A father feels disappointment when his child misbehaves and pride when his child does what is right. A father loves his child through these emotions and exhibits love over all other feelings. I often wonder how one determines which emotions to show, when there are so many being felt at one time. For a father, however, the choice seems to be automatic. A father exhibits the behavior and emotions that illustrate love and understanding, even when he feels sadness. A father feels what the child feels and takes away as much of that pain as possible. A father guides the child to help them avoid pain and suffering and to reduce the behaviors which may cause pain in others.

Discussing the consequences of being a father has led to examining some differences between a creator and a father. God is "the" Father. It is apparent He must experience the same consequences as an earthly father, however on a much larger scale, and for a longer duration, than a mortal father's experience. Fathers feel both the pain their children endure and their own pain and sadness when their children fall or stray from what they have been taught. I have also stated that a father absorbs as much pain and suffering for their children as possible. Does God suffer the same consequences? How could He not? He loves us with a love we could never understand. For God, this is easy as He is love. I genuinely believe He feels our pain and stands beside us when things become difficult. His love causes Him to feel disappointment when we treat each other poorly, and when we turn away from Him. Despite our actions, He continues to show us, love. He does not turn away, and He does not show us His pain. He absorbs our pain and guides us with a father's love.

What did it cost God to offer Himself as our Father? By being our Father, God experiences the painful emotions of humanity. He feels the heartache of a father waiting for cancer to take his child from his arms. He feels the grief of a child being taken away because of changes in circumstances. He wants the best for His children. However, our Lord watches as those children choose difficult paths leading to sorrow. We must ask this critical question, why does He (God) continue to offer Himself and His love?

Listen to Me, O house of Jacob, And all the remnant of the house of Israel, Who have been upheld by Me from birth, Who have been carried from the womb: Even to your old age, I am He, And even to gray hairs I will carry you! I have made, and I will bear; Even I will carry and will deliver you. (Isaiah 46:3-4 NKJV)

God's creation is perfect, including the decision to mold freedom of choice into our existence. With this perfection, however, comes the need for guidance and love in such a way as to provide a glass case that holds His hopes and love for us. Fortunately for mankind, God is not breakable, and He can hold the pain and suffering for all of His children without the glass case shattering.

While I understand that God has entered this relationship as our Father by choice, I am often at a loss when I consider why we rarely emphasize the importance of this decision in our paths through the human experience. Just as it was earlier discussed in this chapter that the terminology we used to express human concepts does not define the role of God as the Father, God is not a father in the mortal understanding of this role, and for that, we should be eternally grateful. Throughout this section of the book, I compared our natural fathers' love and that of The Father, God. Natural fathers love as best as possible, and there is a limit to the love they demonstrate. As limited beings, they try but often fall short. Our heavenly Father does, in fact, love to a much greater degree as He is perfect. The love we receive from

Him is all-encompassing and fulfilling. He protects us and stands by us even when we do the wrong things. However, there is an unfortunate reality in our modern society. Much to our disappointment, not all fathers follow this example of love and acceptance. Consider the number of children who desire a father to play ball with them or take them to the father-daughter dance, then you will understand there is a void in the lives of many children in our culture. There is no greater joy for a child than to have their father present to encourage and provide direction in everyday life. A father must provide unconditional and continuous love for his children and help them feel like they are the most important people in the world. These actions will then become the example a child will need to identify with our Heavenly Father. He does bring an intense love to all of His children. Sadly, this action does not occur in many homes in our world, as many of our children grow into adulthood without any example of love from a father. We need to remedy this action, and soon.

How do we differentiate the role of father to those who experience these questions, and how does this confusion add to the costs that God has experienced by choosing to offer Himself as our Father? These questions have been at the core of this course of inquiry. To this point, I have discussed what type of father stands by his children and leads them through the love of God and through His Word. These are the fathers who share

19

with their children that the love of the Father may be felt forever in their heart. Yet, God sees those who have failed to follow His example. He feels the pain of these children who do not know God's definition of father. He suffers as the children look for a father who will love them unconditionally, and He acknowledges the importance of this guidance here on earth. For myself, had my father not been determined to lead me to make positive decisions for my life, I realize my decisions would have had different results. So, what happens to those children who may never receive this type of fatherly guidance. They may find themselves making mistakes with serious consequences. What happens to the children of those who do not have a father or have never felt the love of a father? What will happen to the next generation of children raised without a father? We must consider the consequences of raising children in a fatherless society. Eventually the children stop looking for a father and fail to seek the love of the Father.

God offered Himself as our Father because He is much more than a creator. He offers Himself as our guide and our protector. He offers Himself as an example of love and how a father should love and guide his children. God revealed His heart to His creation as an example of how we should love. Although there are significant differences in God as the Father and human fathers, there is a peace in knowing that we have an example that could help to reduce the pain and suffering our children will experience. We have the gift of knowing how to love and protect our children by following the example God has provided for us. God is always present and forgiving. God is understanding and compassionate. God is firm in His commandments and certain of His expectations. A father must do the same in order to lead his children to overcome the external influences of the human experience.

As Christians, this knowledge brings about strong responsibilities. So often, we dismiss the importance of a father's role in modern society. A quick scroll through social media will yield multiple jokes or memes about absent fathers. A scan of the news will yield cases of child abuse and neglect. It has become so common that the very term father has lost much of its meaning to the younger generations. As God has given the gift of Himself as our Father, such a shift in understanding of the magnitude of this role creates an even greater sense of grief for our Lord. We must consider how we are adding to this grief by allowing children to grow up without knowing the importance of a father, and for many, believing that this term represents something to avoid. If the children do not know the love of a father, how are they to know to seek the love of the Father? If children are raised to believe that a father can leave or bring them harm, how are they to know that the Father will never leave them and will always provide a shield of protection around them? These questions are essential to the purpose of questioning the cost that God experienced by offering Himself as our Father. The knowledge of God absorbing our pain helps us to understand one of the costs He paid for loving us. I am convinced this action helps us to appreciate the love of the Father more each day. He knows our pains and sorrows!

Second, I would like to turn the discussion to the fathers who are not fulfilling their role to their children as intended by God's example. I believe we must lead the men of our society toward God in such a way they long to duplicate. I am convinced we must illustrate the ways of God as Father as a strong example of how we must carry out our responsibilities. In a society where the roles of men and women have become so complex, a clear exmple is needed. Certainly, women are able to perform the functions of the family, and mothers have proven that they can provide for their children with or without the presence of a father. However, this was not what God intended. Simply because humans can function in a society full of external influences, we must not assume these actions meet the requirements of the Lord. He has carefully given instructions for the best family life. We have given fathers an excuse to avoid leading their children. We have given fathers a way to leave and to fail to follow the example of God the Father. We must change these social norms. We must promote the importance of fathers in the home and lead these fathers to the love of God the Father. In doing so, not only will we be saving the fathers, but also, we will save the children and reduce the suffering that God has graciously accepted as the cost of this gift to His creation.

Finally, we must look into our own experiences in following God's example as our Father. Are we fulfilling our responsibilities in such a way as to reduce the cost of His gift to us? Are we guiding our own children to the knowledge of a Heavenly Father? Do we take the time to train our children in the Biblical principles to enrich their lives? There is a difference in raising a child right and raising them to know God. The difference, I have found, is what the child will do with their own life once the guidance of their father is no longer present. To lead a child to God is to give them a relationship with the Father that will continue to provide love and guidance into adulthood. When we lead our children to God, we believe they will continue to live by His examples, with the hope they will lead their own children to Jesus. The goal of leading our children to God is to reduce the suffering they may experience in this world. As we reduce the physical suffering the child experiences, we are reducing the pain God feels. Our children will experience external influences we have not experienced. As modern society continues to change, these influences may eventually lead our children away from doing what is right. If the children know what is right only in the context of social norms, then they cannot overcome these external influences in their future. However, if they know

God and if they have been led by a father who leads by God's example, then their strength will come from their father. Their behaviors will emulate his. Their love will be complete and given freely to others. They will seek to understand the hearts of others, just as God has allowed them to understand His heart, through their father. They will lead their children to Him, and they will father their children through His example. Are we leading our children to God? Are we leading them by His example? If not, then we are adding to the cost of His offering of Himself as our Father.

In sum, God has offered Himself to us as our Father, as He is more than our Creator. He is the Master Creator, in that all the world came through His idea. He chose what we would become and how we would survive, by creating a world that could sustain our existence. He included freedom of choice into His creation. He knew what would be necessary to help to guide His creation toward making the right decision, while continuing to allow for freedom of choice. He provided the ultimate example as to how each generation could lead the next toward a life that would please Him. He gave the example of how a father should love unconditionally, with both compassion and acceptance. In giving this example, God also loves unconditionally and is ever present. He has shown the world what it means to be a father and how this love changes how the child sees himself and others. Yet, by offering such love and being our Father, God has also formed a path for us to turn our sorrows to Him. He has absorbed the pain and shared our suffering. He feels as we feel. When we follow the example the Lord has set for us, we will lead our children to Him with love and compassion. Ultimately, our actions should emulate the actions of our Heavenly Father. When we are successful in passing on God's love to our children, we may reduce the pain God feels when people are made to hurt by others' actions.

What understanding have we reached through this inquiry? We have explored the nature of a creator and that of a father. We have come to understand God's decision to include freedom of choice into His creation meant there would be changes in how He would respond to His children. He would protect them while also allowing them to be themselves. He will remain present and love them unconditionally, but He will also be firm in His expectations. He will not leave us, and He will never turn His back on His children. He will serve as an example that He wants earthly fathers to follow. He will comfort the children who live without a father, and He will be in the hearts of those who come to Him. God the Father is not an earthly father, and the same modern context cannot be used to define Him. However, fathers who follow His example serve as a light to the children of the world. We must continue to teach our children and those in our community of His love and the importance of the role of a father and of the Father. We must continue to guide our young men to know that they must follow God's example to protect the future generations of children from unnecessary pain and suffering.

But now, thus says the LORD who created you, O Jacob, And He who formed you, O Israel: "Fear not, for I have redeemed you; I have called you by your name; You are Mine. When you pass through the waters, I will be with you; And through the rivers, they shall not overflow you. When you walk through the fire, you shall not be burned, Nor shall the flame scorch you. For I am the LORD your God, The Holy One of Israel, your Savior.... (Isaiah 43:1-3 NKJV)

CHAPTER TWO

Beloved, let us love one another, for love is of God; and everyone who loves is born of God and knows God. He who does not love does not know God, for God is love. In this the love of God was manifested toward us, that God has sent His only begotten Son into the world, that we might live through Him. In this is love, not that we loved God, but that He loved us and sent His Son to be the propitiation for our sins. Beloved, if God so loved us, we also ought to love one another.
(1 John 4:7-11 NKJV)

AT WHAT COST DOES GOD REVEAL HIS HEART?

There was a significant problem in Ephesus. In the year AD 95 (approximately) this once great church had succumbed to agnostic views. Their doctrine stated that Jesus was not the Son of God and was not sinless. This teaching dominated the church at Ephesus, and it is reported that the people called on the Apostle John to help them. By this time, John was the last living apostle, and I am sure he could address this problem. After all, he had spent considerable time with Jesus. It appeared the primary issue was determining whether a person was genuinely saved. John wrote to this church and instructed them to try the spirit and draw a conclusion on Biblical facts and not personality.

When one reads the book of 1 John, there is a

singular pattern developing. Christians are identified by their willingness to turn from sin: *"If we say that we have fellowship with Him, and walk in darkness, we lie and do not practice the truth. But if we walk in the light as He is in the light, we have fellowship with one another, and the blood of Jesus Christ His Son cleanses us from all sin."* (1 John 1:6-7 NKJV) John draws the conclusion that one cannot be a child of God if they walk in darkness or sin. Secondly, John teaches that love is the true identification of the believer. *"He who loves his brother abides in the light, and there is no cause for stumbling in him. But he who hates his brother is in darkness and walks in darkness, and does not know where he is going, because the darkness has blinded his eyes."* (1 John 2:10-11 NKJV) John makes the love factor the clearest identifier. If one does not love their fellow man, they walk in darkness. However, we must ask these questions: Do we know how to love as the Lord taught? Are our best efforts simply fleshly demonstrations of affection? What is the truest model for love?

God has given us a fantastic gift. Through our connection with the Holy Spirit, we may learn more about our Father. As we know the Lord better, we will discover His will and plan for our lives. As we follow along the path of humanity and we fall upon trying times, we do not have to wonder about His compassion and love, but we know of it. When God executes His justice, or we face impossible situations, we know our God is not cruel, but rather, He loves us in everything we go through. He wants to love and wants to be loved by His children. As humans, we often find it difficult to relax in His love and trust His grace. However, when God revealed His heart, we discovered the love of God is much larger than our own issues. In brief, God has revealed His heart as a gift to us to show us not only how greatly we are loved, but also how we should love others, what we should value, and how we should strive to illustrate that we were made in His image.

As we embark on our mortal journey, aiming to hold true to the Master of our image, it is essential to remember He knows us. He knew our hearts long before He revealed His heart to us. Yet, despite knowing us and our hearts, He loved us then as He loves us now. Although mankind continues to fall short of the glory of God, He sees the struggles, and He knows our intentions and our desires. He knows what we face, and He understands how these struggles manifest. He knows how we will respond when obstacles arise on our journey. However, nothing is able to stop Him from showing us His love. Remember, *"For we have not an high priest which cannot be touched with the feeling of our infirmities; but was in all points tempted like as we are, yet without sin."* *(Hebrews 4:15 KJV).* God wants us to know the extent of this love. He wants to share His knowledge with us, and He wants His children to rest in the knowledge of His love and joy. He continues to give of His heart, just as we are to continue to give of our own. To know His heart is to know true love. The heart of God reveals true love. Knowing true love causes us to rest in Him. To show His heart, God has given us the precious gift of love.

The previous assertion leads to an important question and the context of the current chapter. If God has so freely given us this guidance and assurance of His love, what did it cost Him to do so? Certainly, expressing love in a general circumstance may be considered free in that it does not have to cost monetarily, but such considerations do not apply to God. However, when we give of ourselves, this means that a part of us, whether time, emotion, privacy, or otherwise, is now no longer ours, alone. When this occurs, then the consequences are dependent on the value of what has been given. God gave us the knowledge that His love is a love of unending devotion, of absolute virtue, and of compassion for those who are in need. What part of Himself did He give away, and what are the consequences of this gift? This chapter takes us through an understanding of the heart of God. We will then discuss why God revealed His heart. I believe we must understand the costs and consequences of revealing your heart to anyone. Have you ever wondered why the Lord would take such a huge step to reveal His heart to us? Finally, the chapter will close with considerations as to what this perspective means and how we should apply it to our relationship with God.

To begin to understand the costs of its revealing, we

must first discuss what is meant by the heart of God. What a magnificent gift to consider! Firstly, let's consider God in His omniscience, knowing all things about each and every one of us. He knows our thoughts, struggles, sins, as well as our desire to live according to His Word. Over and over again, we are told God knows all, and He knows our hearts. What is even more exciting is we are told He loves us anyway. In fact, because He knows us, He not only loves us but He is willing and able—yearning in fact—to forgive us! How is this possible? This is God's heart, and His ability to know all gives Him the knowledge to understand behaviors and the authenticity of a person's thoughts. In the outstanding statement to the saints at Rome, the Apostle Paul shares insight into this love. *"For I am persuaded, that neither death, nor life, nor angels, nor principalities, nor powers, nor things present, nor things to come, nor height, nor depth, nor any other creature, shall be able to separate us from the love of God, which is in Christ Jesus our Lord."* *(Romans 8:38-39 KJV)*

To put this into perspective, I can recall times in my youth when I would get into trouble. The authorities would call my parents, and they would administer discipline. There were instances when the discipline was physical. Once, when I was being corrected, the cord hit me in the face, and my mother stopped the correction and began to administer healing to the area. You see, while she wanted to correct my behavior, she did not want to scar me. She loved me, and nothing would change that fact! Paul wrote to reassure the believers of the certainty of the love of God.

Even though God knows all and loves all, this does not mean that God approves all. In fact, we are clearly told that God's heart is against oppression. God is a God of justice. *"Speak up for those who cannot speak for themselves, for the rights of all who are destitute. Speak up and judge fairly; defend the rights of the poor and needy." (Proverbs 31:8-9 NIV)*

What an absolute epiphany among mankind. God's heart is not full of love for one set of people or only for those who worship Him. God's heart is full of love and desperate for justice for all of His creation. Does this mean God loves those of different beliefs? Certainly! Does this mean He expects the same of us? Absolutely! The heart of God is fueled by a burning love for the souls of humans. He desires the people come to know Him intimately and with joy. He will stop at nothing to convey the message of His love. The Apostle John teaches us the proof salvation is love. He writes, *"We know that we have passed from death to life because we love our brothers. Anyone who does not love remains in death." (1 John 3:14 NIV)*

Consider the birth of His Son, Jesus Christ, as the foundation of His heart revealed to humanity. Was it only His people who were given the news of the birth of the Savior? No. Instead, the King was welcomed by the Magi, and God repeatedly poured His love onto the Gentiles. God's heart has no room for hatred and no capacity to turn away those who seek Him. Can we each say the same? I remember, early in my ministry, struggling with witnessing to those who I believed, based on personal biases, would not willingly accept my offering of God's Word. If we did not share a common faith, how could we communicate? I knew God said we must love one another, but I also knew He understood the people, and I was not afforded this component of love, a total understanding of others. I admit this embarrassing truth to share how the Lord expects us to move past our prejudgements and love as He loves. It is not easy to love someone you do not know.

How did I proceed? How did I come to love those who believed differently and extend my own faith and love to them in hopes of bringing them into the House of God? I looked into the heart of God. I came to know their stories through conversations with Him and to understand their paths towards faith, challenges, and desires. I asked for His words to be spoken through me and that my heart be filled with His. What happens when we view the world through God's heart? We change our attitudes toward others. We become less condemning and more accepting. Yes, we still have a dislike for sin, and yet we become tender toward the sinner. Jesus taught this lesson. *"So when they continued asking Him, He raised Himself up and said to them, 'He who is without sin among you, let him throw a stone at her first.'"(John 8:7 NKJV)* We must never judge others, as we may be guilty of what we find in the lives of those we judge. The love of God is more accepting and more forgiving than our human efforts. What does this mean? God's heart, in all of its essence, demonstrates just how we are to love others. In fact, true love reveals to us how to love and also how much we are loved.

This leads to the big question as to what it means to reveal. When we look at the most simplistic definition of the word reveal, it is easy to state that the word means to show. However, God is anything but simplistic, and to simply show love would not do justice to the magnitude of His heart. More precious than any material gift, and more beautiful than the aesthetics of any work of art, God revealed His heart! Just imagine! God chose to reveal His heart to us. Through the Old Testament, we rarely see the heart of God in simplicity. In many instances, we are forced to interpret what He meant in the passage. In most cases we are woefully wrong, and that is because we lack the heart of God to make the true love decision.

I remember the challenge of revealing myself in adolescence. If I were to fit in, then I would have to appear to be just like everyone else. I would have to talk like the others and dress in the same style. I actually studied the interests of others so that I could discuss these topics at the "cool" lunch table. I managed to fit in quite nicely, and the mirage was received by all of the others who, I now assume, were doing much the same thing. I could not simply open myself up to potential critique, because that could leave me alone and on the other side of the cafeteria. I could not possibly reveal myself and my interests. Yet, although I was surrounded by my peers, I was alone. I was absent from myself in such a way that I did not know how to return.

Eventually, I decided to let my true self come out.I expressed myself and learned that I was right all along. Revealing myself led to a greater sense of isolation, but I found a calmness that I had never known. I was finally okay with myself. During this time of change, when the voices of all of those I thought I should listen to became quiet. I was then able to hear my own voice and the voice of God. The Psalmist encourages quiet, reflective thought. He instructs us, *"Be still, and know that I am God: I will be exalted among the heathen, I will be exalted in the earth." (Psalms 46:10 KJV)*

I was able to better understand how He had been shut out by so many simply because He revealed Himself. He expressed a love so great that most people could not understand, and many found it easier to turn away from what they did not understand rather than embrace this great love.

When I thought about this more deeply, I realized a sense of sadness in the world could quickly be addressed if the world would simply accept what God has revealed. If the world understood the love in God's heart is real and everlasting, then people who feel alone and isolated would be able to know God is with them. They would come to realize He not only understands them but also accepts them. Much of the pain that has become the norm through the human experience would be diminished if humans would receive the love of God. People will experience a much higher sense of peace, in much the same way as I found a calmness, when they drop the masks of life and are true to themselves and the Lord God. It is difficult to understand why so many choose to ignore the realities of God's heart and the magnitude of His love, but it is even more challenging to understand why so many people refuse to demonstrate His love to others. I am reminded of an experience that I witnessed within a congregation. I believed this congregation truly understood the heart of God. I felt the love of God in such a way, it seemed to overflow from the windows and doorways. Yet, as I thought about the greatness of this love, I was reminded of another fact. Along with our earthly bodies comes prejudices and misunderstandings. So often, man is fearful of what is not understood.

On the particular Sunday morning of worship, a young couple, dressed in what I can only imagine would be worn to a nightclub, entered and sat at the back of a church I was visiting. The young woman, who appeared to be in her late teenage years, looked to be around six months pregnant. The young man, also appearing in his late teens, had several visible tattoos, as well as uncombed hair and a poorly managed beard. The couple did not speak when they entered but rather sat quietly in the chairs throughout the service. There was no indication they were familiar with the church, as they did not stand when others did, nor did they bow their heads during prayers. They simply sat and observed, and when the service concluded, they continued to sit right there in the back pew of the church. Very few spoke to them, and I have often wondered how the people could allow this couple to slip out of the church without inviting them to return. What did the people miss as this couple sat through the worship? Were we afraid to talk to them about our dear Lord? How could we show the heart of God to someone who really needed and may have been, in fact, looking for that warm touch? What had drawn them to the chapel that day, and what had they needed from us that we did not provide? When we do not understand, we look away. When we are fearful, we shut down. When we fail His people, we fail God.

Yet, God knows we do not see things in the way He does. He understands when we do not fully grasp the intents of the heart of another person. He fulfills the needs we fail to meet. In His heart, there is no room for fear or doubt. In His heart, there is only love for all of His creation, and therefore, even though we failed, He knows this young couple is seeking Him. The type of clothes they wore or the style of their hair does not keep the Lord from loving and walking toward them with the greatest gift ever offered to humans. Salvation! Time and time again, I have spoken with God about this couple and others that I allowed to slip into eternity without a word about Jesus. He has assured me He forgives me, and He continues to love me. He continues to reveal His heart to someone like me! It is breathtaking to know even though we fail, He will continue to love us. Yet, regardless of how deep and everlasting this love is, man continues to turn God away. Man fails to seek the love God has provided. That is, of course, until a challenge becomes too difficult or the loneliness becomes too great. Only then is man able to hear the voice of God. When the rest of the world seems to be so loud, it becomes possible to slip away and just listen. What is then heard is the heart of God!

When we know of God's love and His heart, then we know how we should love others and live as the light of the world. When we know God does not hold His love only for those who worship Him but instead maintains a place in His heart for all of His creation, then we can open up to others and share His love without biases, misconceptions, and fear of rejection. By revealing His heart, God did not merely give us a command to love, but also instructions on how to treat others.

I believe God knew revealing His heart to His creation would have consequences and costs. However, He also knew of the circumstances we would face where we would need His help of love. How could He expect mankind to follow His example, if the example was not provided? If He had simply instilled unconditional love for others into His creation, we would not need His example of love and care. However, His creation includes freedom of choice, so He chose to ensure that all options were clear, including the option to exhibit love for others. What did this cost Him? By opening His heart of love, the Lord places Himself in the position of feeling our pain and loving us when we sin. His very nature is holy, and He has little tolerance for sin. However, when He opened His heart of love towards us, He gives His mercy over judgment. God could have easily shielded His heart and commanded His creation to be kind to one another. He could have loved unconditionally without opening up His heart for the world to see. Yet, the Lord wanted to show such compassion that it would flow from His Spirit into the hearts of mankind. This majestic love is demonstrated to the whole of humanity through the death of Jesus on the cross. This action resulted in the greatest gift given to humanity. To prove to the world how much He loves us, God gave His Son as the ultimate sacrifice. *"For God so loved the world, that he gave his only begotten Son, that whosoever believeth in him should not perish, but have everlasting life. For God sent not his Son into the world to condemn the world; but that the world through him might be saved." (John 3:16-17 KJV)* This demonstration of the love of God fully illustrates the cost of revealing His heart to His creation. When we evaluate the heart of God, we reach some conclusions that may be different than those we thought all of our lives. The demonstration of the love of God costs Him everything. He had to turn away from His Son and watch Him become sin for us. This is a powerful example of love.

I often think about the way our God shows His love toward us. As I grow older, I have come to realize that all actions have consequences, and although God knows all, each decision He has made regarding His creation has also come with some sort of effect. I have often considered the outcome if the decisions we made had been different. For example, have you ever taken a moment to review your friendships in your youth? What would have happened if you had chosen a different place to sit in the cafeteria on that first day? Would you have been more focused on your studies or found yourself going down the wrong path? Did you ever wonder why you loved a certain person and not another? What would have happened to your life if you had made another decision? My mother would often tell me of the story of how she met my father. She said she was on the number three bus and she saw my dad on the bus. She asked a friend if she knew who that good-looking man was sitting there. Well, the friend introduced them and now—well, let's say I am now here. I give that illustration to suggest the fact that every decision has a motive and a consequence. When the Lord chose to open His heart and show His love, what was the motive? I believe the motive was to draw us closer to Him. God does not want to be a stranger. He consistently invites us to come to Him and share His presence. He even says that He inhabits our praise: *"But thou art holy, O thou that inhabitest the praises of Israel."* *(Psalms 22:3 KJV)* I think the consequence of this love is the fact that God may get hurt. There are many passages of Scripture illustrating the feelings of God. He can be grieved and He often felt sorrow for His children. God could have insulated Himself from these emotions, yet I believe He wanted to be the example of what true love is all about. I am sure you have come to realize this reality: love hurts! So, it seems our God chose to hurt for us and with us. When we sin and disobey Him, we hurt Him.

Every decision that we make leads to the next, and each has consequences. For myself, I have often wondered what happened to those who I failed to share the Word of God. Indeed, God did not hesitate to share His Word and His love, but I considered the consequences of rejection and felt as if I could not bear what could happen. After all, He knows all now, and He knew all then. But do we consider the cost when we think of the magnitude of this gift of God? Imagine—God opened His heart, became the example of magnificent love, and knew He would get hurt in the process. He knew His creation would not consider His heart when they made decisions and performed actions contrary to the heart of our Father.

Some people behave differently when they discover

43

your real heart. It is a shame when people use your strengths against you and take your kindness as a weakness. I feel we often exhibit this behavior with the Lord. As I thought about this issue, I came to understand how we often take advantage of knowing God's heart. There is a passage that often brings me to tears. *"I called for my lovers, but they deceived me: my priests and mine elders gave up the ghost in the city, while they sought their meat to relieve their souls."* *(Lamentations 1:19 KJV)*

The Lord is calling for those who say they love Him, to enter a deeper soul relationship, but they go after what pleases their flesh rather than what honors Him. We know He loves us, and we know this love is all-consuming. He has such compassion for us and He wants nothing more than for us to come to Him for help and direction. Granted, we may not come to Him willingly. We may avoid His care at times; however, I do not believe we do this knowingly—at least not intentionally. I can think of more than one occasion when I have avoided His care as I succumb to the pressure around me for the moment. I am sure others share this mentality. Some people think the love God has for them allows them to have extra time to repent. Unfortunately, this is not always the case. When the Lord reaches out to us, we must respond immediately. His expression of love does not always include more time on this earth. When the Lord sends someone to share the message of love, we must remember our time does not translate into God's time. Remember, the love of God reaches out to us at the hour we most need it. We may not have time to respond at a later time. Paul teaches, *"We then, as workers together with him, beseech you also that ye receive not the grace of God in vain. (For he saith, I have heard thee in a time accepted, and in the day of salvation have I succoured thee: behold, now is the accepted time; behold, now is the day of salvation.)"* (2 Corinthians 6:1-2 KJV)

So, at what cost does God reveal His heart to His creation? From my interpretation, He did not give up anything that was not replaced. I believe the Lord wanted us to experience the power of love and forgiveness daily. Since there was no other example of this love, He filled us with His love, with the hope we would live by those principles exhibited by the Lord Jesus. He knew that some part of His creation would take advantage of the magnitude of His love and choose to embrace it in the last moments of their mortal lives, which, although His heart burns for souls, would mean that these people would have had many lost chances to spread His Word. He knew this, and yet He loves us, and so He revealed His heart, a heart of full compassion and care.

In revealing the heart of love, God hopes people will fully understand that no action against God will cause His love to waver and therefore use this knowledge as a crutch upon which they can justify their behaviors. Still, others will ignore the magnitude of God's heart, as they are unable to grasp such a love that is unconditional and unending. They will not be able to fully understand God does know them better than they themselves and He loves them despite their flaws and failures. The apostle John teaches, *"Behold what manner of love the Father has bestowed on us, that we should be called children of God! Therefore the world does not know us, because it did not know Him."* *(1 John 3:1 NKJV)*

God feels the loss when these people do not feel His love and turn away from Him. God feels sadness when people neglect to follow His example, treat others with less love than has been shown by Him. He feels the pain of those who cannot understand His love despite His clear examples. God revealed His heart, intending to guide His creation to be loved and to love others. So many do not follow this guidance, and it has cost God a sense of loss for the souls that have not come to know Him and His enduring love.

Why did God decide to show His heart to His creation, knowing that many would not use this knowledge for good and that many would not follow His example in loving one another? Why did God reveal His heart to His creation, knowing that He would still watch His creation follow a path of destroying others rather than bringing them into His light? Why? Because He loves us. He loves me, you, and all of creation. We may never fully understand this love here in Western culture. Our idea of love is based on what a person does for us—how they make us feel, and what we can get from them. However, from the biblical perspective, true love is not measured by what we receive, but by what we give.

What are we to do with this knowledge? How do we move forward, knowing God willingly paid this cost with consideration of His own pain? Personally, I believe each time we reconsider the magnitude of this gift, God is joyful. I think every time one person, a single soul recognizes He loves them so much. God is satisfied. I believe we are meant to learn of His love not only through Him showing His heart, but also through others who have learned to follow His example. I hope, in some way, through my own confessions of revealing how I have both failed and learned, you may somehow also come closer to genuinely emulating the heart of God. What a glorious world we would have if we loved others as God loves us. Think about how different our lives would be if we simply accepted others as God accepts us. We would have a life of joy if we forgave others as Christ forgave us.

When Jesus was asked about the greatest commandment, I am sure the response confused the more religious listeners. With over 300 laws to keep, how would it be possible for the list to be narrowed to the one most important? The answer given by Jesus speaks to the heart of God. His answer was so simple, and yet the answer reveals the heart and mind of God. His answer, "The first of all the commandments is: 'Hear, O Israel, the LORD our God, the LORD is one. And you shall love the LORD your God with all your heart, with all your soul, with all your mind, and with all your strength.' This is the first commandment. And the second, like it, is this: 'You shall love your neighbor as yourself.' There is no other commandment greater than these." (Mark 12:29-31 NKJV)

I can only imagine the faces in that crowd. No mention of Mosaic or Pharisaical law, just a simple instruction to introduce the Kingdom of God through the attitude of love. The heart of God is all about loving people. Walking in this love and practicing forgiveness is a great gift. I recall an instance in prayer when, as I talked to God, I began to boast about how I treated people. I said, "Lord, I treat people as I want to be treated, as I keep the Golden rule." His response shocked me as I heard Him say, "No, my son, I want you to treat people the way you want me to treat you!" Believe me, His instructions sure changed things in my mind. We are to reach people with the love of God, not our love. Would it not be easier to spread the love of God if we did not view this gift as power over God, but rather the power over hatred and judgment on earth? Could we not more freely speak of His love and His heart if we also illustrated their magnitude through our own actions and interactions with others? I would like to believe this is the reason God decided we were worthy of the cost. He knew we would eventually understand what we were to do with this wonderful gift of His love.

As God looks upon His creation, He sees His children. He has opened up His heart and revealed the majesty of His love. He has shown His children how they should love one another and how they should try to understand the journeys that others endure, despite the differences of their backgrounds. He has provided extensive examples of what it means to love unconditionally, as He loves each of us. He has never wavered in that love, despite what behaviors we may exhibit. Yet, God sees us when we bring harm to others. He knows when we act in such a way that does not reflect His teachings. The Psalmist declares, *"The eyes of the LORD are upon the righteous, and his ears are open unto their cry."* *(Psalms 34:15 KJV)* He feels the pain others feel due to our selfish actions. He cries tears for those who call out to Him when they are not treated fairly by others. He looks upon His creation, and knows He has taught every person the way of love, but many choose to avoid those lessons. He feels disappointed when these examples are not followed. He gave His creation the power to make choices. We must be careful to treat people with the same love and consideration as God would treat them. We must not allow external influences to overpower His teachings and His examples.

Moving forward, we must understand an important fact. God gave us the gift of revealing His heart, and this gift came at a cost to Him. He could have directed our actions without giving us the example of knowing just how much He loves us. He could have provided us with an innate ability to overlook the external influences and to focus only on the joy of love. He could have removed these external influences and allowed only love to flourish. However, God did not create us in such a way that we do not have choices. In fact, the removal of the ability to chose would result in a race of robots. I am so happy God did not want us to be like robots. This was not God's design. His design is perfect, and He understands we will experience the world in a way unique to each of us. Yet, just as mortal parents, God feels for each of His children. He feels our pains, and He sees the pains that we cause. Therefore, He has shown us the way out of this darkness. He has shown us to love others means we must try to understand their hearts. We cannot simply recognize the external influences; instead, we must carry in our own hearts the love and compassion that God has illustrated by revealing His heart. God is love, and He wants us to know how powerful His love truly is to all who need to feel this love.Without seeking His heart, we are lost to the external world and we cannot live in His example. Revealing His heart would expose our Lord to the pains His creation would inflict upon others. Yet, He did so, knowing many would seek Him and follow His example of bringing love to others and helping them come into a relationship with Jesus.

What have we learned through this line of inquiry? Personally, I have gained a much stronger sense as to why God decided that it was necessary to reveal His heart of love to His creation. Certainly, God has such a power that He does not need to convince His creation to live in His way. He does not have to open up His heart to benefit others. Yet, He chose to do so in order to provide an example of how He expects each of us to love one another. He opened His heart for us to understand how powerful love is and how it can heal others. We cannot see into the hearts of others, and that causes us to misunderstand the actions we see. However, God can look beyond the surface and look into the hearts. He has given us the directive to try to understand the reasons people behave as they do. Love does not look at the physical actions only. Love does not take offense, but it looks to mend and forgive. We have learned in doing so, God revealed He loves us unconditionally, and this knowledge is often used by His creation as a way to justify some actions of disobedience. For example, there are moments in our lives when we disobey the Lord. Have you ever found yourself thinking about the love and mercy of God and how it will cover the sin? Have you ever taken the love of God for granted, knowing He will forgive you for the offense? This was the cost for God to reveal His heart. He knew some would overestimate His grace and underestimate His judgments. He knew this, and still, He reveals His heart of love. What a mighty God we serve! He loves us, and He understands our behaviors, but He continues to expect us to live a better life and love more in the way He demonstrates to all of us. This beautiful gift to us must not be taken lightly, but rather should serve as an example of how we must treat others. As we love others, we show God our love for Him. Then we become the reflection of His love for all of humanity. When people question God's love, they should be able to look at the lives of the Christian and find the proof they need.

One of the more popular songs sung by Dionne Warwick is titled "What the world needs now is love." In my view, the words of that song speak to the heart of God. Love works, and we need to try this formula of the Kingdom of God. The Apostle Paul tells the church at Corinth that love is the best result for life. He teaches the Kingdom principles of love. He writes, "Love suffers long *and* is kind; love does not envy; love does not parade itself, is not puffed up; does not behave rudely, does not seek its own, is not provoked, thinks no evil; does not rejoice in iniquity, but rejoices in the truth; bears all things, believes all things, hopes all things, endures all things. Love never fails. But whether *there are* prophecies, they will fail; whether *there are* tongues, they will cease; whether *there is* knowledge, it will vanish away." (1 Corinthians 13:4-8 NKJV) Paul further discusses the eternal concepts of love. He teaches in verse thirteen: "And now abide faith, hope, love, these three; but the greatest of these *is* love."

When confronted by the lack of maturity in the church at Ephesus, John the Apostle teaches the lesson about love with the same passion as Paul. He tells the people about the power of love. John says we must love our brother and if we do not we walk in darkness. When we walk in love we walk in the light of God. He who loves his brother abides in the light, and there is no cause for stumbling in him. But he who hates his brother is in darkness and walks in darkness, and does not know where he is going, because the darkness has blinded his eyes. (1 John 2:9-11 NKJV) These passages are designed to answer the principle question at Ephesus. The question asked was as follows, how can we tell if someone is truly saved? John says by watching for the demonstration of love. We may place emphasis on good teaching and preaching, faithful church attendance, and the like. John, however, says love is the master key. Only children of God can walk in true love and demonstrate the power of God through love. The writings of John speak to the possibility of being in church and yet not walking in love. As I discussed earlier, the love of God is shed in our hearts in order to have us love as the Lord loves.

Someone once said, the proof of the pudding is in the eating. I feel the same way about love. Love is not a feeling; it is a demonstration, and it is an action. It is the proof of being filled with the Holy Spirit. Paul writes, "But the fruit of the Spirit is love, joy, peace, longsuffering, kindness, goodness, faithfulness, gentleness, self-control. Against such there is no law." (Galatians 5:22-23 NKJV)

The best passage for our conclusion is found in Paul's

letter to the Ephesians: *"That Christ may dwell in your hearts by faith; that ye, being rooted and grounded in love, May be able to comprehend with all saints what is the breadth, and length, and depth, and height; And to know the love of Christ, which passeth knowledge, that ye might be filled with all the fulness of God. Now unto him that is able to do exceeding abundantly above all that we ask or think, according to the power that worketh in us, Unto him be glory in the church by Christ Jesus throughout all ages, world without end. Amen."* *(Ephesians 3:17-21 KJV)*

CHAPTER THREE

For this cause I bow my knees unto the Father of our Lord Jesus Christ, Of whom the whole family in heaven and earth is named, That he would grant you, according to the riches of his glory, to be strengthened with might by his Spirit in the inner man....
(Ephesians 3:14-16 KJV)

AT WHAT COST DOES GOD HAVE A RELATIONSHIP WITH HIS CREATION?

Relationships are tough. You put your trust in someone and hope they will love you for who you are and do their best to bring joy into your life. We humans often struggle with relationships. It seems only fitting that we look at the relationship we have with the Lord God. Have you ever wondered why He wants to be in a relationship with us? There are times when we hurt Him and fail to obey His directives, yet He continues to chase us and attempt to bring us into harmonious relationship with Him. As young Christians, the concept of God brought fear. We were very much afraid that He would kill us if we did the wrong thing. We were always told God wants HOLINESS! Holiness was a thing always out of reach, and we were doomed because we could not achieve it. We were taught that removing ourselves from certain activities and modes of dress would promote Holiness. Our walk with God was inundated by fear. If you did wrong, you might miss the Rapture and go to hell. Yes, we were never told about the relationship God wanted with His creation, let alone the fact that He wanted a relationship with us.

"Hear, O Israel: The LORD our God is one LORD: And thou shalt love the LORD thy God with all thine heart, and with all thy soul, and with all thy might. And these words, which I command thee this day, shall be in thine heart...." (Deuteronomy 6:4-6 KJV) This passage tells us God wants love from His children. He cries out to be connected and become more than an idol to His children. What does it cost to enter into a relationship with someone? Many have discovered the lie of love. Here is what I mean—the lie of love is "I love you as long as I feel good about myself, as long as you do for me, as long as you do not find anything that is not the best about me." Loving relationships are always costly, and before we enter into any relationship, we must discover just what the relationship will cost.

I believe we must consider what relationships cost God. At what cost does He dare to enter into a relationship of eternal magnitude? In fact, the Lord has stated, "I will never leave you, nor forsake you." (Hebrews 13:5)

Never, Lord? Never? What a testimony of character. I am sure we have all had someone in our lives who promised they would never leave us, and the shoe dropped. They left you, stopped calling you, and abandoned the position they held in your life. I am glad our God does not dismiss us so easily. He promised He would never leave us. No matter how messed up we become, He stands beside us to bring us comfort and hope. Our question makes reference to the cost of this relationship. As with anything concerning the Lord, His word is His bond. If you have a promise from God, you can depend on Him to keep it. *"Heaven and earth will pass away, but my words will never pass away." (Matthew 24:35 NIV)* What a marvelous promise.

When the Lord makes a promise or gives a word, we can rest on it and never fear those words going unfulfilled. All relationships with the Lord are built on a promise, and the promise will be fulfilled in Him. This leads me to an interesting passage in the book of Deuteronomy. After the children of Israel cross the Red Sea and prepare to enter the land of promise, the Lord gives a relational warning. He tells them to beware of one major thing: *Beware that thou forget not the LORD thy God, in not keeping his commandments, and his judgments, and his statutes, which I command thee this day: Lest when thou hast eaten and art full, and hast built goodly houses, and dwelt therein; and when thy herds and thy flocks multiply, and thy silver and thy gold is multiplied, and all that thou hast is multiplied; then thine heart be lifted up, and thou forget the LORD thy God, which brought thee forth out of the land of Egypt, from the house of bondage."(Deuteronomy 8:7-14 KJV)*

You see, God always runs the risk of losing some of His children to the blessing He gives us. This action plays out at times in our personal relationships. When someone has a person in their lives who is good to them and treats them with loving exceptional treatment, in many cases the relationship may turn sour. Why? Because some people cannot handle being treated in a loving manner. If they had someone who was mean and heartless, they tend to stay with that person. God risks His relationship with us when He blesses us. I believe this is the reason He says when you are blessed, DO NOT FORGET ME! I think one of the most painful experiences of life is to be forgotten by someone who said they love you. Once again, the Lord waits for this love and connection, to be the result of creatures with freedom of choice. I wonder why?

Our God is a mighty God. He is all powerful and can command His creation to behave in such a way as to please Him. He is above all and greater than all. He does not need from us and there is nothing more that we can offer Him beyond our loyalty and love. His power and strength are beyond what we could ever understand, and we are helpless without Him. Yet, He chose to know us! He chose to have a relationship with us! For the longest time, this concept seemed so vague. Generally, a relationship involves giving and receiving so that all needs are met. Friendships provide companionship and support. Family provides love and nurturing. The idea of a relationship where only one party could truly provide for the other seemed strange. Why would God want to have a relationship with His creation when He already knows our limitations? In order to answer these questions, we must first consider what it means to have a relationship and how different relationships vary in the contributions of each party.

I considered the relationship that one has with a friend, as God is our friend and comforter. He offers His companionship to us and we offer, in return, our devotion. How do we choose our friends? So often, we become friends with others out of mere convenience. *"A friend loves at all times, and a brother is born for adversity." (Proverbs 17:17 NKJV)*

In my youth, my best friend was my neighbor, because he was always available to spend time with me. We had an understanding about one another's family life and we were able to spend as much time as we wanted together, because our parents knew one another. While I am thankful for having this childhood friend, we did not maintain our closeness as we aged. In fact, we were nearly strangers when we last spoke. Today, I view friendships not based on convenience but rather on common interests and goals. When we choose our relationships with friends based on commonalities rather than convenience, then the relationships can last beyond space and time. We add to one another's journey by providing knowledge and support. We aim to understand how the other person's life is different from our own, and we share our own perspectives without expecting that they view the world in the same way. We seek to understand rather than to change. We offer help and communication when necessary, yet we do not pass judgment when wrong decisions are made. We offer forgiveness and compassion. This is how the Lord treats us. He is consistently with us, and He offers comfort and encouragement. In fact, one of the greatest things the Lord said to His disciples is as follows: *"No longer do I call you servants, for a servant does not know what his master is doing; but I have called you friends, for all things that I heard from My Father I have made known to you. You did not choose Me, but I chose you and appointed you that you should go and bear fruit, and that your fruit should remain, that whatever you ask the Father in My name He may give you."* (John 15:15-16 NKJV) Friendship is important.

I then considered the relationship between a child and their parents. This relationship is not as give and take as one that is chosen, such as friendship. Parents provide for their children's needs and offer love and support. Children offer a sense of continuity and love to their parents and, in many cases, a loyalty to their values. However, this is not always true. Parents do not always provide, and children do not always follow the rules. Yet, the relationship between the two remains strong. I remember my mother telling me that no matter how old I became, or what I did with my life, she would continue to be my mother. She explained that she might not always agree with me and that our goals and interests might differ, but that she would be my mother for eternity. In other words, nothing could change the fact that she will always be my mother. Is it possible to have an association so strong without also having a relationship? Are the dynamics of a birth relationship stronger than a relationship of choice? What I have learned is every relationship is determined by the circumstances surrounding it. It does not matter if the relationship is by birth or by choice. How we fulfill our duties in the relationship is what really matters.

So, what does this mean for our relationship with God? As our Creator, He is able to choose the dynamics of the relationship and what He expects in return. He is able to choose if the relationship will continue and how it will serve to determine how we view Him and others. When considering the two types of relationships presented, I have determined that God's choice to have a relationship is based on the common goal of reducing suffering and the association of Him as our Father. In the book of Malachi, God asks a question of the children of Israel, and I believe this question is still relevant today. They had strayed far away from the Lord. Their hearts had grown so cold towards the Lord, they even with-held their offerings. When the prophet writes to them, the question is just as piercing today: *"A son honoureth his father, and a servant his master: if then I be a father, where is mine honour?" (Malachi 1:6 KJV)* What a great question. Children must honor their parents all the days of their lives. In our current culture, the honor reserved for our parents is missing. As a result, parents are dis-honored, and their guidance is rejected. The command-ment tells us to honor our mother and father all the days of our lives, and we will have long lives as a result. God is saying, if I am your Father, where is my honor?

For a parent, their child's accomplishments and their love are valued. For children, they look to the parents to provide for their survival needs and nurturing through their developmental stages. They seek support and guidance, and the relationship is dependent on the value that they place on their parents' contributions to fulfill these needs. Here, it is possible to better understand why God chose to be in a relationship with His creation. While I was able to identify what we contribute as minimal in comparison to what He offers to us, He places a much higher value on our contributions of love and loyalty. He places a high value on our obedience and willingness to follow His di-rections. He gives to us life, love, and salvation—and yet, He values our contributions as joyful to Him.

Is there always an equal share of contributions in a relationship? Unfortunately there are times when the contributions are not equal. Certainly, one can see that these contributions are considered equal when the value that is placed on each element is significant to the recipient. God values our love and fellowship because He gave us free will, and therefore, we can choose to avoid His presence to a degree. God could have demanded that we follow Him. The Lord could have made us without freedom of choice. Then He would have had the devotion of all of His creation by default. However, this would not have been a relationship. This would have been the association of a creator and the creation. This is not what God wanted for us. Instead, He wanted to know we would follow Him and love Him without force. Can you imagine the children who feel their parents only provide for them because they have to do so? These relationships fail, and ultimately dissolve. God wants an eternal relationship with those who seek Him. Jesus expresses this idea in two places in the Gospel of John. Jesus speaks of how permanent our relationship with Him becomes, He says, "All that the Father gives Me will come to Me, and the one who comes to Me I will by no means cast out." (John 6:37 NKJV) And again He references the permanent relationship; He continues, "And I give them eternal life, and they shall never perish; neither shall anyone snatch them out of My hand. My Father, who has given *them* to Me, is greater than all; and no one is able to snatch *them* out of My Father's hand. I and *My* Father are one." (John 10:28-30 NKJV)

God cannot get rid of us, based on His character and promise. Praise the Lord! He cannot abort any of His children. This is one relationship that is eternal.

Relationships often end for reasons we do not understand. It is comforting to know God will never end His relationship with us. He is eternal, and He will continue to contribute to our lives in such a way as to achieve the goals of reducing suffering. He will work within the realm of our free will to guide our paths toward Him and into the Kingdom of Heaven. God does not leave us. However, all too often, we leave the Lord for things soon to evaporate. All too frequently, external influences make us question our relationship with God. More times than I care to count, I have seen a member of the congregation sitting in the pews, not knowing that this would be the last time that they would be in attendance. Some of these people begin what I call the journey of the Prodigal Son. They take their blessings from the Lord and leave Him. Their fellowship begins to deteriorate, and they lose the joy of serving the Lord. Even though they attend church faithfully, they lose connection with Christ. What happens to make them leave their relationship with God? How is it so easy to walk away from a relationship with Him, as He gives far more than we could ever offer? Do we forget the importance of the eternal presence of the Lord in our daily lives? Do we forget the importance of our common interests to our human experience as well as our eternal presence? While I understand there are reasons mutual physical relationships end, I have yet to understand how we can justify turning away from daily fellowship with God.

Can you imagine offering your friendship time and time again, knowing the other party will continue to turn away from you? Could you continue to accept them, or like most of us, would you eventually come to terms with the reality that the relationship was over? Thankfully, God never accepts the end of the relationship as His reality. God continues to work to regain the bond between Himself and His children.

He waits for us to return, and when we do, He welcomes us with open arms. He shows the same unchanging love for us, which has always been in His heart. I often wonder why the Lord continues to reach out to us. We pull away, and He reaches out, demonstrating so great a love for all of us. Our Lord will always respond to our pleas of forgiveness and restoration. He is right there when we seek Him.

There is calm confidence in knowing our Lord will always respond with mercy and forgiveness. Peter the Apostle reminds us of a truth spoken by Joel: "And it shall come to pass, that whosoever shall call on the name of the Lord shall be saved." (Acts 2:21 KJV) This passage reminds us of the promise of God hearing us when we call out to Him. The motivation for the response is simple, God loves us! He has provided us with the knowledge that He will not turn us away if we seek Him. What does this mean? Does God experience the loss of His relationship with each person who turns away from Him in the same way? Certainly, as God desires this relationship, the loss would bring Him sadness while the continuation of the relationship would bring Him joy. Expressing a desire to maintain a relationship with His creation, therefore, cost God the experience of grief.

Let us consider the two types of relationships that have been previously discussed. In the first relationship, God is viewed as one to be served and feared. Obedience was the primary contribution expected of us, while God offered the provisions to meet our daily needs. Humans had free will and could choose to disobey God, but these choices were met with swift consequences. There was little room for doubt concerning the power of God and how He wanted to be served. So we see the first type of relationship was built on fear and a view of God being able to destroy and judge us. This type of relationship did not bring us into His presence with love. God looked upon His people and realized there was still something missing. Something which could only be satisfied by a strong relationship with Him. His creation needed a way to know Him in order to drive their internal desire to serve Him. As He demanded to be obeyed, the exhibition of free will was restricted. This was not the intention of His design. God, therefore, sent His only Son to serve as a sacrifice to illustrate His commitment to the relationship that He desired with His creation. The second relationship was fueled by the desire of the Lord to have His children come to Him and love Him willingly. The Lord knew we had to have a sacrifice to pay the ultimate price to bring us into a pure, open relationship. The sacrifice was Jesus, and through His death, we enter into a better relationship of family and spiritual connection. When Jesus died for us, God offered a way to avoid the eternal consequences of sin. Through the sacrifice of Jesus, we were now able to enjoy the blessings of the Kingdom of Heaven, even here on Earth. The life of Jesus demonstrated how much God wanted obedience and how much He loves us. This new direction offered peace through salvation and a feeling of belonging to the family of God. What a tremendous blessing to receive! To achieve this new relationship, God not only sacrificed His only Son, but He also gave His children the knowledge they could return to Him if they fell away.

We must understand this fact, our obedience to God is essential to maintaining this relationship. As we grow closer to our Lord we begin to realize what this relationship cost Him in order to be close to us. God could have easily developed a relationship that demanded obedience and responded with immediate consequences for those who disobeyed. After all, He is the master and we are His servants. Although the Lord loves His creation, His love would not have been emphasized through the type of relationship which forces the creation to serve the creator. We were lacking in our ability to love Him willingly.

The old relationships had to change. I do not believe the Lord wanted to be viewed as a God who punishes at random. The Old Testament gives the image of a consuming fire, a God who kills for any violation of His law. As we move into the New Testament, we see the Lord wanting to share our lives, and we come to realize this fact; His judgment is but for a moment, but His mercy endures forever. I believe this is the reason Christ was given to us and for us. We needed to see the heart of God and not just His actions. He would bring His children home through revealing that He was willing to pay any cost to have this relationship with them. Yet, the cost did not end there, as we continue to fall short of pleasing Him. When we turn away from Him, He grieves. When we fail to communicate, He is saddened. When we choose to disobey, He is disappointed. These actions of restoration continue to define the relationship God desires. Through the actions of mercy and grace, He keeps us from complete failure.

When I think back on a time in my life when my father wanted me to call him more frequently. He told me, "Rick, just call to say hello." I never knew this little conversation was important, so I just began to call him every day and say, "Hello, Daddy." It made a world of difference. Just as my father just wanted daily contact with me, I suggest our Heavenly Father desires daily contact with us. Remember, the key to any relationship is communication. He could force us, but He would rather love us into submission. Without daily contact, how can we know the joy of our relationship with the Lord? Is it possible to grow in Him and avoid talking with Him regularly? Even as external influences pull us away from our time with Him, we are continually drawn by the Holy Spirit into fellowship.

So how do we use this information to minimize the cost of God entering into this relationship with us? How do we fulfill our contributions to Him? The relationship we now have with God replaces the Old Testament model. We walk in love, and we trust Him from the inside. With the indwelling of the Holy Spirit, we are given more insight into the heart of God, and that knowledge should strengthen our walk with God. We must still obey God. As we obey Him, then we also please Him. This is our Creator, our Father, our Protector, our Comforter, and our Master. He is our God and He not only demands, but also, He deserves to be obeyed. Obedience not only pleases Him, but it also prevents much of the suffering we see in our modern society. When we follow our fleshly instincts, or those presented by external influences, we fail to recognize the principles of God and we fall short of His values. We dismiss what He has asked of us and what He has commanded us to follow. One of the greatest assets of our new relationship with the Lord is that we do not have to suffer eternal consequences for our sins. When we are adopted into the family of God, He washes our sins away, and we realize a new peace and joy in Him. We must be careful when evaluating our new relationship and never think God's mercy will allow for willful disobedience. I do not think we should sacrifice mercy for obedience. In times past, God has shown His power and His anger for our actions, and He can undoubtedly repeat those actions. We must remind the next generations of the need to obey and submit to the will of God. Yes, He is a compassionate God, but He also expects that we obey Him. Only through this understanding will His children come to Him completely trusting in His will.

Next, God is a jealous God. He has made it abundantly clear that nothing else shall be placed before Him. We all know there are times when His children choose other relationships over their relationship with Him. The result of these decisions can lead to anxiety and the loss of the joy of the Lord. We must put Him first, in much the same manner as He has continued to put us first. This is the reality of our relationship with God, the Father. He must be first. There can be no excuse for those who leave His side for temporary pleasures. When the children of God seek other relationships apart from Him, He feels the pain of abandonment. Indeed, we celebrate when people return to the Lord, just as He rejoices. However, we must realize this fact; forgiveness is not an indicator of acceptance of the actions exhibited by His children. When the Christian becomes a "prodigal", God patiently waits for them to come to themselves and seek Him afresh. The cost of His mercy is allowing us to run amok at times. He does welcome us back into fellowship, but the relationship is still intact.

We know God desires a relationship with us, and it brings Him joy for us to know Him. It brings Him joy when we talk with Him, seek Him, and obey Him. We must put Him first and love Him with all of our heart, mind, and soul. These actions become our contribution to our relationship with the Lord God. While we must try to bring others to His love, we must not waver in fulfilling these contributions. As we do so, we will serve as an example of His Way, Then others will see the joy we have in our lives and the peace we enjoy in our relationship with Him. If we do not illustrate joy in our lives, which comes naturally through our relationship with God, others will indeed look away and not seek Him. Our constant obedience and dedication will serve as a return on the costs He paid to share His love with us.

I hope we have a greater understanding of the cost to have a relationship with the Lord. We note the changes in the relationship God seeks with His children. These changes are designed to remove the fear of serving the Lord. In the Old Testament, God is viewed as a God of judgment and destruction. Since the birth, life, and death of Jesus, we can see our Father as a God of mercy and grace. I do not want you to be confused. God is still holy and righteous, and He will not clear the guilty. However, he does love His children, and His desire is to bring us together with Him. We have discussed the sacrifice of His only Son, Jesus Christ, as a means to illustrate how significant this relationship would be to God. God gave Jesus as an illustration of His love for us; he knew we were incapable of producing the life He desired. We must remember the passage in the Gospel of John, "for God so loved the world that He gave His only begotten Son, that whoever believes in Him should not perish but have everlasting life. for God did not send His Son into the world to condemn the world, but that the world through Him might be saved." John 3:16-17 (NKJV) He showed us He understood we want to please Him, but with the gift of free will, we often go astray. Therefore, He offered us a way to avoid the consequences of these sins and to be welcomed into the Kingdom of Heaven. This expanded the relationship between God and His children, as He not only wanted us to obey, but He also wanted us to know Him and to talk with Him. He showed us He would never leave us, no matter how many times we turned away from Him. This came with the cost of grief, as those who choose other relationships before their relationship with God leave Him. We must lead others to His way and continue to share the importance of obeying Him and putting nothing or no one else before Him. We must continue to hold up our end of the relationship. The responsibilities we have are as follows; obedience, spending time with God and sharing the good news of His kingdom. When we do these things, we will continue to serve as an example of the gift of relationship God has given to His children.

CHAPTER FOUR

*For God so loved the world, that he gave his
only begotten Son, that whosoever believeth in
him should not perish, but have everlasting life.
For God sent not his Son into the world
to condemn the world; but that the
world through him might be saved.*

(John 3:16-17 KJV)

AT WHAT COST DOES GOD GIVE HUMANITY SALVATION?

The Apostle Paul encourages the church at Corinth with these words: "Thanks *be* unto God for his unspeakable gift." (2 Corinthians 9:15 KJV) He gives the thanks to God for His unspeakable (indescribable) gift. I believe Paul references both Jesus and salvation. God wanted to save His children, and He was deliberate in giving the greatest gift to humanity. Salvation is a substantial gift to all. But what was the cost? We examine not only the Christological concept, but also the spiritual applications. When God gave His Son, He gave all of Himself. The cost was tremendous. In childhood, we are taught every action comes with consequences. In some homes, the consequences may be more severe than in others, with extravagant rewards for doing what is right and corporal punishment, such as paddling, for exhibiting bad behaviors. These consequences serve as reinforcement for the values and morals that the parents aim for the children to uphold. Gradually, children become fearful of negative consequences. Parents can only hope this attitude will help the child avoid bad decisions and embrace those attitudes and behaviors, leading to better consequences. When they see the rewards for obedience and hard work, they may become motivated to do better. We have discovered this universal fact, all actions have equal or opposite reactions and consequences. We can only trust the Lord to lessen the resulting consequences for our actions. This simple principle continues into adulthood, with consequences ranging from a raise at work to incarceration, depending on the type of behavior. In the mortal realm, therefore, there is no way to escape consequences.

However, this is not the reality of our spiritual existence. Here, I want to discuss what is meant by the term salvation. In the general sense, salvation is the principle of being saved. In the Biblical sense, salvation is the principle of being saved from the consequences of sin. To trace this backwards, yes, there are consequences for every action, and the consequences for sin are severe. Yet, through salvation, these eternal consequences can be avoided and the sins can be forgiven. *"There is therefore now no condemnation to those who are in Christ Jesus, who do not walk according to the flesh, but according to the Spirit. For the law of the Spirit of life in Christ Jesus has made me free from the law of sin and death." (Romans 8:1-2 NKJV)* Through the gift of salvation, God has given us a path to His Kingdom in Heaven as a reward for accepting this gift. This changes the course of our eternity! All humans sin. The magnitude of these sins varies, but we all fall short of the Glory of God. We experience life as mortals, and therefore we experience human thoughts and emotions. We respond to these emotions through human behaviors. Even as we try to live in obedience to the Word of God, we often fail. Sadly, we fail at times without even being aware of our failures.I remember a sermon by an evangelist that focused on the importance of always asking forgiveness for sins. He said we should always repent of sins we know about. That is a good piece of advice, but what about those sins we do not know about at the time? The work of the Holy Spirit is to identify those personal shortcomings and give us enough light to come to the Lord and confess all things to Him. We are human, and we sin. *"If we say that we have no sin, we deceive ourselves, and the truth is not in us. If we confess our sins, He is faithful and just to forgive us our sins and to cleanse us from all unrighteousness. If we say that we have not sinned, we make Him a liar, and His word is not in us." (1 John 1:8-10 NKJV)* To clarify, salvation is what was missing from the human experience. As mankind sought to please God, they became painfully aware that they would continue to fall short of His Glory and that, regardless of what was in their hearts, they would continue to sin, leading them to suffer eternal consequences as well as to suffer here on earth. While we were in this state, there was no hope to avoid eternal suffering. Our Lord had to step in and give us hope. What a feeling it must have been to realize, no matter how much you loved God, you continued to fail Him and there was no way for true redemption from these sins. *"As it is written: there is none righteous, no, not one; there is none who understands; there is none who seeks after God." (Romans 3:10-11 NKJV)*

How fearful His children must have been to know their souls would be punished for their sins long after their suffering on earth had ended. Yet, God saw this sense of desperation. God saw the fear we had regarding eternity. Would we go to hell or would God weigh our good against our bad and we can just make it into Heaven? Our Lord saw our desire to do what was right, yet we lacked the ability to live according to His standards. He knew He had to make a change. He had to make a way for His people to live in peace and find their way home to Him. He knew He had to offer a permanent way out of eternal damnation. He had to offer eternal salvation.

Without the gift of salvation, we would have no hope of a better life beyond this earthly one. Imagine living a miserable existence here on earth, then dying and going to hell, and ultimately the lake of fire. It took the Lord to step in and fix this problem. He helped by offering us the gift of His son, Jesus. The death of Jesus guarantees a better life in eternity.

Salvation is a gracious gift from the Lord. The price is more than we could ever pay, and the Lord gives this gift to us freely. While He does not force salvation on anyone, He uses situations to drive us to the inevitable fact, we need Jesus to live a decent life and then go to the Kingdom of God when we leave this world. Jesus is the only way to God, and His death paid for our sins. This gift, while free to us, came at a high cost to the Lord God.

He sent His only Son to suffer and die for us. As a father, I cannot imagine sending my only child to die for people who do not love me. In fact, I could not send my child to die for those who liked me. Give the gift of salvation to people who ridicule your name? Save those who use every opportunity to violate your instructions? Only the Lord God could make this decision for us. What a mighty God we serve. The Lord knew Jesus would be the only way out of sin and shame. He also knew many people would not come to Jesus. Many would have contempt for the Lord and avoid surrendering their lives to Christ. Jesus would lead the people to the feet of God and bring them peace. However, this was to be a sacrifice made with the blood of Jesus. He must shed His blood and die for us. The cost of salvation was more than we could ever know. He gave His Son to die for us, so we could avoid eternal damnation. Hallelujah! He knew His Son would suffer in such a way that would bring justification to those who came to Him. His Son would have to suffer to such an extent that it would wash away all of the suffering that His creation would bring to one another. The blood of His Son would have to be spilled in order to provide a way for the sins of His creation to be washed away. He knew the pain and suffering of His only Son would be so severe, He would have to absorb it into His own essence. He knew all of this, and yet He sent Jesus to bring us the gift of salvation.

Jesus Christ did not simply live among mankind; He lived as mankind. Raised in an average family, Christ was able to experience life in the same manner as everyone. He understood what it meant to be without and to desire something more. However, He knew why these moments of suffering were necessary. *"For we do not have a High Priest who cannot sympathize with our weaknesses, but was in all points tempted as we are, yet without sin."* (Hebrews 4:15 NKJV)

Jesus understood His Father's plan. He knew that He had to teach the principles of the Kingdom of Heaven. He must successfully reveal God as a loving Father who cares for our well being. Jesus also knew what was expected of Him, as He was to be our ultimate example. John the Baptist identified Jesus as the Lamb of God to take away the sins of the world. Jesus understood the sacrificial lamb and how He must take on that unique role. Jesus also knew He would be sacrificed as a way to bring God's people home to the Kingdom of Heaven. He saw the hatred and the pain creation experienced, and He tried to alleviate as much of this suffering as He could while He walked the Earth. Jesus knew we would be able to apply the truths of the Kingdom when we are exposed to suffering. He would help us through our times of suffering while being there to help us endure. What a mighty God we serve. He may not take the suffering away, but we learn to overcome the suffering and walk in victory. What a chore to place on a single individual! Teach them and love them, but also be prepared to die for them! Christ, however, was not fearful because He knew the human presence was only temporary. Jesus provided an example for all to follow. He was totally focused on the will of God, and He would not allow anything to keep Him from His destiny. The most important task was to get to the cross and die for all humanity. Hallelujah to the Lamb of God!

And so, God watched as Jesus was met with extreme cruelty and hostility. The suffering and death of Jesus was an extreme act of violence. God could have provided a path to His Kingdom, which did not require such a violent death for Jesus. However, if He were to make salvation pain free, I wonder if we would have appreciated the costs? The events leading to salvation had to be as significant as the outcome; eternal salvation and life with God. So, He watched as His Son was treated cruelly. He watched as the soldiers did everything they could to break Jesus. The situation was so difficult, Jesus even told His followers, " I could call my Father, and He would send twelve legions of angels." He took the pain of the cross and endured the shame so we could have eternal life. Then God watched as the body of our Lord was placed in a tomb and covered with a stone. God watched, and He felt every hurt His Son felt. But, then, He rolled the stone away and lifted His Son back to the Kingdom of Heaven to show His creation He can and will do the same for all of His children. The Lord made it clear we do not have to face this world alone, and He understands the struggles we face that could lead to sin. He watched as His own Son's blood was spilled on that cross, to tell us that His blood could wash our sins away. He gave us the power of salvation! "But as many as received him, to them gave he power to become the sons of God, even to them that believe on his name: Which were born, not of blood, nor of the will of the flesh, nor of the will of man, but of God." (John 1:12-13 KJV)

I have often considered why God made the sacrifice of His only Son to illustrate the path to Heaven. Even more, I have wondered why God offered us salvation. After all, we are sinful, in that we are influenced by our human experience and make decisions through the gift of free will that do not always reflect the Will of God. We sin and God sees these behaviors. He knows our thoughts, as well as our hearts. We cannot hide our sins from God. To look upon His creation, having given everything necessary to survive and flourish in His Light and to witness so many behaviors that go against His Way, must certainly bring Him sadness and disappointment. He would clearly have been justified in turning us away from the Kingdom of Heaven. The Lord wanted to give the gift of Himself. He is so holy, He could have turned away from us. However, He extended His love to us in such a way as to call us into His family. He wants to fill the Kingdom of Heaven with His children. He chose to sacrifice His Son and to allow Him to suffer, so we would finally see how much the Lord cares for each of us.

Salvation is not simply being saved in the present; it is the knowledge that this protection lives on through Jesus Christ. This comes with the knowledge that, despite the conditions of the human experience, we have been washed, and God awaits our presence in the Kingdom of Heaven.

The difference between salvation and forgiveness has often been one that is difficult to explain. When God offered salvation, He removes the eternal consequences of our sins. This action is far greater than forgiveness. Granted, forgiveness is included in this magnificent gift, but salvation is much more than accepting an apology. In fact, salvation is difficult to understand in the mortal environment. I remember hearing someone state that "everyone seems to find Jesus in prison. He must spend a lot of time there." While I understood the context, as they were discussing how many people claim to have found salvation in order to improve their chances of approval at their next parole hearing. Our day-to-day lives often are so loud that it is difficult to hear His voice. I can imagine there is a lot of time to listen in prison, so one may hear the voice of the Lord more clearly. God offers forgiveness for the sins or crimes, and He offers protection from the eternal consequences of sin. However, mortal punishments or consequences are different.

So, if salvation does not necessarily reduce human suffering or protect from mortal consequences, what does this gift provide to His children? Salvation offers hope for an eternal future. The sacrifice of Jesus does impact our present life. However, the real impact is for the future. Have you ever looked at a family who seems that they can never catch a break? The father struggles to earn enough money, the children often fall ill, and the mother has taken on so many responsibilities, she is unable to care for herself and her family. The adverse situations this family faces continue to grow. However, despite the difficulties, this family remains peaceful. They continue to stand not merely from a position of hope; they have peace. They have learned hope is different from peace. Hope is a sensation one feels when they want something to happen or to receive something. Peace, on the other hand, is knowing what is to come.

Although this family suffers at present, they have peace knowing they are born again believers in Christ. They know they will be received into the Kingdom of Heaven. They can endure the suffering of this present world as they wait on the arrival of their Lord, Jesus. They do not have to simply hope they will be received by God; they know salvation is a gift of God with no possibility of loss. They do not rely on hope; rather, they live in peace. Knowing He gives us freedom from the consequences of our sins and, through the blood of His Son, our sins can be washed away gives us peace to confront the issues and conditions of the mortal world. To live in God's love is to live in peace, and that peace comes through the gift of salvation.

When I think of what it means to have peace, I am firstly drawn to the quiet mornings when I am alone with God and talking with Him. I do not think of the busy day ahead or the things that must be completed. I do not rustle through the house to make certain that everything is ready for the day. There is time for that later, and these tasks will be easier to complete once I have taken this time with Him. At times, I pray for those who have reached out to me for prayer, and I talk to God about what I know about their circumstances. Other times, I just read over His Word and listen to Him. I know this is our time together, and the peace surrounding me will be with me throughout the remainder of my day. I know there will be other moments throughout the day when I will feel the need to talk with Him about things He wants me to know. However, in these morning moments, I step away from my routine to talk with Him. I have discovered mornings are essential to the Lord. We should spend time with Him before we are polluted with the cares of the world and trivial matters designed to interrupt our connection with Jesus. Yes, my friends, in these early morning moments, nothing distracts me from Him. These times bring the most peace. Just being able to step away from the daily routine of the day may bring a degree of peace for those who long for His peace. The ability to sit in silence and have nothing on the mind to interfere with the peace and calm moments is the fruit of salvation. Still others define peace as a simple knowledge that everything is going to be okay. I do not believe any of these actions are wrong, but all reflect the gift of salvation. When we know God, then we know the beauty of every moment. When we talk with God, we know everything will be okay. When we receive salvation, we have nothing to fear.

For those of us who have known the peace of God for most of our lives may find ourselves taking it for granted. It might be possible to enjoy this peace but not realize this relationship with the Lord is not something possessed by everyone. I am saddened when I cannot bring others to this place of peace.

How could they choose to suffer eternal consequences for their human experiences when God had given them the gift of salvation? Yet, we must continue to be available. We must know God has a plan for each life. We must work in His name but understand that each person must seek Him for themselves. They must listen to His call to salvation and respond. How it must grieve the heart of our Father when His creation refuses the call to a better life. I have peace in knowing I spread His Word to all those I encounter. I know many of His children do not hear these messages, and others store them in their hearts for later. For those who respond and enter a relationship with the Lord, peace comes alive in their hearts and minds. When they come to the family of God, I celebrate and rejoice in His name. I thank Him and worship Him, as I know I have lessened the costs He has paid for my salvation and yours.

We know the gift of salvation is essential to mankind, so we must fully understand God's cost to provide such a wonderful gift in our human experience. The most apparent cost we must examine is the suffering of His only Son. Although we know Jesus Christ was raised from the dead and lives on alongside His Father, we also know He suffered greatly here on earth. Can you imagine looking into the face of your child and telling them you love them, but you must send them to suffer so that others may also know your love? Can you imagine having the ability to protect your child from all of the pains of the world and yet choosing to send them to not only suffer as human, but to suffer a fate more painful than most would ever experience? God sent His Son as a beacon of light to illuminate His love for His children. He sent His Son to shine this light to all of mankind without prejudice or discrimination. Yet, He was met with such prejudices and denied by those who refused to acknowledge the power of God. Over and over, His Son taught of His love and the ways to live in accordance with Him. Time and time again, God observed as His Son was refused, chastised, and treated with hostility. Each time, God could have called Him home, as I am certain we would all want to do for our own children. Yet, God had a plan. When the Romans hammered the nails into His Son, God saw the pain His Son felt. He absorbed this pain and suffered with His Son. When the blood of His Son poured from the body of Jesus, the Father knew salvation could be offered to His creation. He knew the suffering of Jesus would lead to peace with God for all who would accept this precious gift. He gave His Son as the ultimate price for our salvation and our peace.

The costs endured by God are not limited to the sacrifice of His only Son. While this ultimate cost is enough to show God loves us so completely that He will accept any cost to bring us to Him, the fact remains many do not seek Him. Others live hoping an opportunity for salvation does not come with a time limit, as they live out their lives in sin, in the hope, there will be enough time to seek Him before they leave their mortal existence. This is often evident among young adults and adolescents

There is not always time! We are not promised to

wake up in the morning. Diseases, natural disasters, accidents, and violent actions continue to take the lives of our young people. Have we done enough to show them the need to seek salvation when it is presented? The people must know the only way to come into the Kingdom of Heaven is to receive the gift of God, Jesus Christ. Are these people exhibiiting sinful behaviors because they believe they have time to come to the Lord in their later years? It is in this reality that God suffers. He offered an open invitation to have our sins washed away. He gave His only Son so we might know the way to Him and be protected from the eternal consequences of our sins. The Holy Bible teaches we must seek the Lord while He may be found and call upon Him while He is near (Isaiah 55:6). However, so many of His children fail to seek Him before it is too late. As God clearly wants His children to return to Him in Heaven, the cost of offering this gift is the knowledge many will not receive it. Could He have compelled (forced) us to seek Him and receive the gift of salvation? Certainly, in His all-powerfulness He could have approached salvation in this way. However, as it has been asserted, God created us with free will and to take that away would be to alter His creation.

Are we warning others with a sense of urgency that they seek salvation to live in peace and celebrate in the Kingdom of Heaven, or are we allowing them to think there is always time? When we fail to bring His children to Him, then we are adding to the cost that He has paid for our salvation. When we allow the youth to pass from this earth without knowing God the Father, then we are condemning them to suffer the eternal consequences of their sins. As God has saved us from these consequences, we must guide others to receive the same gift.

The gift of salvation is the most remarkable gift God has given to us. He chose us because He loves us, but He also knew the costs. The Lord knew we would fail at times, and in the worst case, we would just disobey His instructions. The Father was willing to accept these costs because He knew some of His children would be lost for eternity. He had to offer them a way to escape the eternal punishment of hell. Salvation through Jesus is the only way to come to God. What a wonderful God who loves us so much He would pay the ultimate cost to secure our place in the Kingdom of Heaven! How could we possibly deny God's love? Certainly, these gifts do not come without obligations. We cannot merely seek salvation and then turn away from God whenever we decide we have had enough. We must continue to stay the course of obedience and remember our only hope is in Christ. As humans, we sin daily, and we must seek His forgiveness without fail. Our primary responsibility is to love God with all of our hearts and our neighbors as we love ourselves (St. Mark 12:30-31). We must follow His way of illuminating love to the world that He has created for us. When we fail to maintain a relationship with God, then we miss the full potential of the gift of salvation. What joy we discover from daily walking with the Lord. We know our eternal position is secured, but we find contentment as we walk with the Lord. I must warn you, you should not wait until tomorrow to begin this relationship, (For He says: "In an acceptable time I have heard you, And in the day of salvation I have helped you." Behold, now is the accepted time; behold, now is the day of salvation. (2 Corinthians 6:2 (NKJV) We must acknowledge this fact, every day on earth could be our last. We must not think there will be enough time to turn to God as time is not promised to us. We must begin and end each day by seeking Him and His forgiveness. We must stop throughout our day and seek His guidance. We must talk with Him and listen to His voice. However, there are conditions to receiving salvation. First, we must believe Jesus is the only way to God. Second, we must believe we are all sinners and condemned to hell. Third, we must confess our sins to the Father and ask His forgiveness. Jesus gives us a promise, "all that the Father gives Me will come to Me, and the one who comes to Me I will by no means cast out." John 6:37 (NKJV).

What have we learned from seeking an understanding as to what it cost God to offer His children salvation? I believe that the highest cost was the suffering of His only Son. However, I also believe that it is the loss of those who wait to receive these gifts that often bring sorrow to Him. Many people in this world are unaware of the precious gift of peace, which comes along with receiving the gift of salvation. Many live without hope and peace simply because they believe they will always have time to come to the Lord. Sadly, this is not always true. There are so many who do not seek Him. These individuals are unable to hear the voice of the Lord. The Apostle Paul teaches why this happens. He says, "but even if our gospel is veiled, it is veiled to those who are perishing, whose minds the god of this age has blinded, who do not believe, lest the light of the gospel of the glory of Christ, who is the image of God, should shine on them." Corinthians 4:3-4 (NKJV) This brings Him sadness. This is especially true when there is not enough time. We must continue to spread His Word and do so with a sense of urgency that is so often omitted from our sermons. Today is the day to seek salvation. Tomorrow may be too late.

EPILOGUE

I have written this book to help you understand that salvation, while given freely, is certainly not cheap. Our culture has pulled us away from the fruitful relationship our God has prepared for us. We have become so at ease in this world that we have forgotten the basic desires of God. He wants to fellowship with us and give us life.

In the African-American church, the image of God is one that elicits fear. We have heard about a God who is mean and cruel. He (we are taught) holds us to standards that rob us of joy and in fact, the harder our "grace," the holier we are. We are often made to feel we are hopeless in our desire to please Him. We are taught to be so afraid of God and do not question Him on any level. We are constantly reminded that we must be different, but we have no joy in our salvation.

My pastor, the late Reverend Benjamin Smith Sr.,

used to tell us, "God gives us a little bit of Heaven to go to Heaven with." I liked that saying. We should be the example of joy and peace. It is time to break out of the prison of church and the religious attitude of the Pharisees. We should be joyful children of God. We are adopted into the family of God, and our lives on Earth must reflect the love and joy of God. After all, our Father paid a tremendous price to bring us to His family.

I pray you rediscover your joy after reading this book. God has given much to adopt you, and you should rejoice now that you are no longer an orphan. So I encourage you to relax and enjoy the life of God and walk in the victory He has given. Blessings to all!

"The LORD bless thee, and keep thee: The LORD make his face shine upon thee, and be gracious unto thee: The LORD lift up his countenance upon thee, and give thee peace." (Numbers 6:24-26 KJV)

CPSIA information can be obtained
at www.ICGtesting.com
Printed in the USA
BVHW072339060221
599331BV00001B/7